𝔚𝔬𝔩𝔩𝔞

ℌ𝔞𝔲

Family House and Natural History Museum.

by Elizabeth May, M.A.

ISBN 0 946404 02 X

2001

The Nottinghamshire Heritage Series

Walk & Write Ltd
Unit 1, Molyneux Business Park,
Whitworth Road, Darley Dale,
Matlock, Derbyshire. England.
DE4 2HJ

'Lovely art thou, fair Wollaton; magnificent are thy features. In years now venerable thy towery-crested presence, eminently boldly seated, strikes the beholder with respectful awe.'

Throsby's Thoroton.

CONTENTS

To my parents, and to the memory of Eric, a dedicated supporter of the Willoughby family and Wollaton's heritage, former member of staff at the Natural History Museum, Wollaton Hall.

INTRODUCTION

The Elizabethan stately home of Wollaton Hall, built for Sir Francis Willoughby between 1580 and 1588 and surrounded by beautiful parkland, provides a fitting setting for the county's Natural History Museum. From the grandeur of the building and its dominant hilltop position, it is easy to see why it was originally designed to be one of the finest homes in England and a fitting residence for one of the county's great landed families.

The Willoughby family were descendants of a wealthy Nottingham wool merchant, Ralph Bugge, who purchased land at Willoughby-on-the-Wolds during the early 13th century. His grandson, Sir Richard de Willoughby, married Isabella, the sister and heiress of William Morteyn, owner of extensive lands at Cossall and Wollaton. As a result of this marriage in the mid-14th century, the Wollaton estates came into the control of the Willoughby family.

The 16th century was a profitable time for this rising family, who gained increasing wealth through trade and prosperity with status by important marriages during this period. Henry Willoughby, father of the builder of the hall; Sir Francis married Lady Anne Grey, daughter of the Marquis of Dorset, and Sir Francis himself married into the Lyttleton family. During the early 17th century, another Francis, his grandson, was awarded a knighthood on his marriage to Cassandra, the daughter of the Irish Treasurer, the Earl of Londonderry, whose descendants controlled extensive coal mines in County Durham by the 18th century. Although certain Willoughbys were knighted due to their various personal achievements, the family did not acquire a title until 1677 when Francis, elder son of the Naturalist, was made Baronet in recognition of his father's achievements. His brother Thomas who succeeded him was made Lord Middleton by Queen Anne in 1711. Thus, by the late 16th century the family had become very prosperous having acquired ownership of large estates in the Midlands, London and the West Country and also renown as industrial magnates due to the success of their coal mining exploits in the Nottingham area.

It is ironic that coal mining, generally regarded as a spoiler of the landscape, should ultimately lead to conservation, which has become the function of the modern day Wollaton Hall. The Hall is situated in the area of a coalfield and it was the very profits from this industry which allowed Sir Francis Willoughby to afford to pay for the building of this lavish stately home. Inevitably, such indulgences led to the accumulation of extensive debts during the latter part of his life.

Sir Francis, however, was not the only Willoughby of renown. Others used the very prosperous period during the 16th century in order to fulfil their own personal ambitions. Sir Hugh Willoughby, for instance, turned his attention to adventure, and exploration, rather than settling for aesthetic glories like Sir Francis. Such achievements by the family in their long history contributed greatly to the prestige of the village of Wollaton and the surrounding county of Nottinghamshire. However, it was not until the rise to prominence of Francis the Naturalist in the mid-17th century that the Willoughby family and Wollaton Hall became associated with Natural History. By this time, the financial problems incurred by Sir Francis, the builder of the Hall had, by careful management, been rectified, enabling the family to resume the life of leisure associated with such stately homes. This ultimately provided an opportunity for Francis the Naturalist to undertake extensive travels in Europe, and with the help of the botanist John Ray, to become a famous pioneer in the field of Natural History. Although most of his studies and research took place at Middleton Hall in Warwickshire, where he spent much of his life, Willoughby made frequent visits to the family residence at Wollaton Hall, and it was to Wollaton that his books and collection of specimens were transferred after his death in 1672.

Since its sale by the 11th Lord Middleton to the Nottingham Corporation in 1925, the Hall has functioned as a Natural

History Museum, working together with the Nottinghamshire Trust for the protection of local wildlife. The importance of this would probably not have been recognised, but for the work of Francis Willoughby who compiled detailed records of the discoveries he made on his travels. These were to be invaluable to future generations. One feels that it is wholly appropriate that this stately home, with its lands previously used for hunting, should now be devoted to nature conservation.

The following extract from the Willoughby family tree shows the more notable Willoughbys and their immediate families.

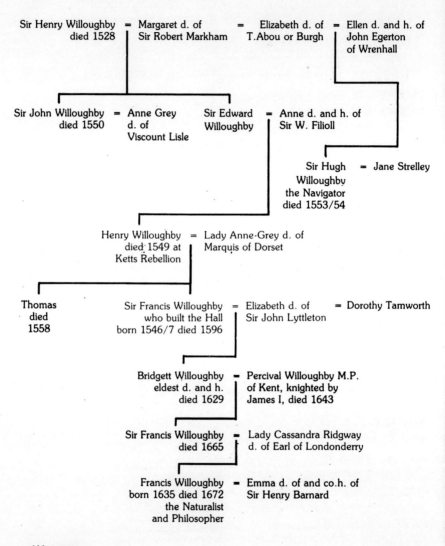

Sir Henry Willoughby = Margaret d. of = Elizabeth d. of = Ellen d. and h. of
died 1528   Sir Robert Markham   T.Abou or Burgh   John Egerton of Wrenhall

Sir John Willoughby = Anne Grey   Sir Edward = Anne d. and h. of
died 1550   d. of   Willoughby   Sir W. Filioll
  Viscount Lisle

Sir Hugh = Jane Strelley
Willoughby
the Navigator
died 1553/54

Henry Willoughby = Lady Anne·Grey d. of
died 1549 at   Marquis of Dorset
Ketts Rebellion

Thomas   Sir Francis Willoughby = Elizabeth d. of = Dorothy Tamworth
died   who built the Hall   Sir John Lyttleton
1558   born 1546/7 died 1596

Bridgett Willoughby = Percival Willoughby M.P.
eldest d. and h.   of Kent, knighted by
died 1629   James I, died 1643

Sir Francis Willoughby = Lady Cassandra Ridgway
died 1665   d. of Earl of Londonderry

Francis Willoughby = Emma d. of and co.h. of
born 1635 died 1672   Sir Henry Barnard
the Naturalist
and Philosopher

Abbreviations:
d. — daughter
h. — heiress

WOLLATON HALL AND ITS TRANSITION

Wollaton Hall is both representative of the wealth and prestige of the Willoughby family and also stands as a landmark to their achievements in the field of Natural History. Originally built as a stately home and designed to be one of the most architecturally innovative buildings of the age, it stands as a monumental tribute to its builder, Sir Francis Willoughby. Although the Hall's purpose was to change in modern times, its grandeur was to remain and its landscaped surroundings and spacious interior make it an ideal centre to display the wonders of Natural History and the work done in this field today.

Sir Francis Willoughby, the builder of the present day Wollaton Hall, was an ambitious man and had wealth enough to live a life of leisure. However, he led an unfulfilling life and managed to squander virtually all the family fortunes prior to his death in 1596. Sir Francis was descended from the Marquis of Dorset and was first cousin to Lady Jane Grey, the 'nine days Queen of England'. However, despite his ambition and noble position, he had an essentially weak character and was easily taken advantage of, both in business and his personal life. The Hall was, in fact, the only ambition he actually fulfilled and only then by going into debt. His personal life was beset with problems and his two marriages, despite giving him seven daughters, failed to provide him with a son and heir. The first marriage to Elizabeth Lyttleton resulted in an expensive divorce settlement around 1587. His second wife, Dorothy Tamworth, in the words of Thoroton, 'made advantage of the declining time of her husband and his estates.'

At the beginning of the 1580s with extensive estates to his name and some highly profitable coal mining ventures, one can understand Sir Francis's decision to use current income to finance the building of the Hall. The early pits at Cossall had been extended to include mines at Wollaton, Bilborough and Strelley by the late 15th century. They were at their most prosperous during the 1580s and providing yearly profits in excess of £1,000, the Wollaton mines suffered a substantial decline later in the decade. Unfortunately other major industrial ventures he invested in during the 1570s, including a scheme to grow and process woad, an ironworks and experiments in the manufacture of glass, were not as successful as Sir Francis had hoped. Extensive land purchases in the Nottingham area together with great personal expenditure, generated a financial crisis, which almost extinguished the Willoughbys as a gentry family.

Sir Francis had no son and heir, and thus Wollaton Hall was to provide him with a memorial both to his position and wealth and also acts as a reflection of his ostentatious nature. Indeed, the 'cri de coeur' date stone over the south door portrays the life of this man perfectly with its 'Behold this house of Francis Willoughby, an unhappy, heirless, but ambitious man.'

The north facing main entrance of Wollaton Hall   Photograph: Elizabeth May

10

The Hall is situated on rising ground, giving a beautiful view of the surrounding countryside. Its prominence must have appealed to Sir Francis's nature and its position was fully exploited by the architect Sir Robert Smythson, to whom we attribute the design of such houses as Longleat and Hardwick Hall.

Wollaton Hall took eight years to build using stone from quarries at Ancaster in Lincolnshire, and was completed in 1588, the year of the Spanish Armada. Various investigations conclude that the total estimated cost of the building would have been £8,000, though Cassandra Willoughby in 1702 claimed the figure to have been an astronomical 'four score thousand pounds.' Up until its completion, Sir Francis had been living in the Willoughby residence in Wollaton village, to where the family had moved in 1450 from Willoughby-on-the-Wolds. In 1575 Queen Elizabeth I was invited to visit another Willoughby residence, Middleton in Warwickshire. Evidence suggests that she declined and perhaps it was this which inspired Sir Francis to build a more lavish home five years later.

Wollaton Hall represented one of the latest innovations of the age, both structurally and stylistically, with its blend of the Medieval, Flemish and Italian classical architecture. It was one of the first houses structured for aesthetic as opposed to defence purposes. To the modern reader it may appear ostentatious, however, this together with its original design very much appealed to the romance of the age. Wollaton differs from earlier Elizabethan mansions due to its spectacular total symmetry, its unusual raised Central Hall and Prospect Room. In the design, Smythson left behind the conventional Elizabethan E, H or L-shaped arrangements to create something new, a house structured around a central hall. The influence of French designer du Cerceau, who later inspired the famous Palladio, is evident from the overall shape of the Ground Plan.

As a building, Wollaton Hall has a great dramatic intensity and a quality of animation. The recession of the facades, wide corner pavilions and complex ornamental detail all contribute towards the spectacular overall impression. In order to create this visual effect, Smythson drew a corner of the house in

11

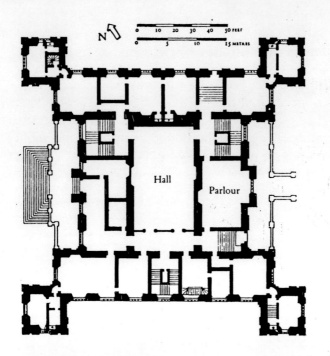

Above: **The Ground Floor Plan of Wollaton Hall desiged by Sir Robert Smythson**

Below: **A plan taken from J. A. du Cerceau's *'Petites Habitations '* (1560) found among the Willoughby papers, which with its central hall and corner towers almost certainly provided Smythson with the inspiration for the Wollaton design**

Acknowledgement to Mark Girouard's book *'Robert Smythson and the Elizabethan Country House'* (1983) and to the R.I.B.A. London.

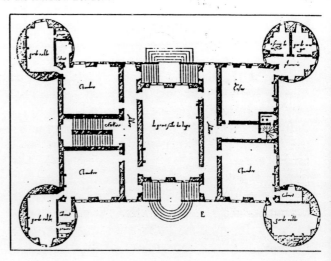

perspective. This remains the earliest surviving perspective drawing by an English architect.

The exterior of the Hall bears a definite resemblance to Longleat, an Elizabethan mansion with an Italian influence built during the 16th century. As J. Summerson states, 'the resemblance is mainly structural and confined to the elevations, lying in the perfect symmetrical design and also on its horizontal emphasis by means of wide stone bands extending over the facades.' Like Longleat, it too has a great quantity of windows, which are surrounded by classical pilasters with both Doric and Ionic capitals. 'Other classical

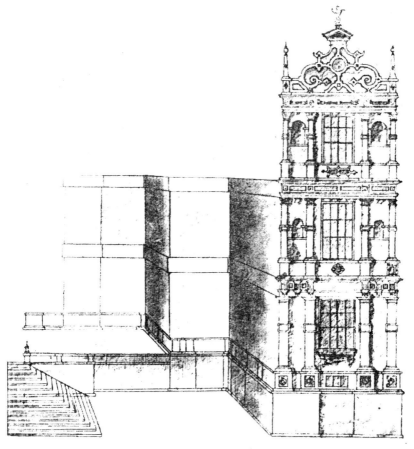

The Smythson perspective drawing demonstrating the recession of the facades at Wollaton
Acknowledgement to R.I.B.A. London

features can be found adorning the central bays of the East and West fronts, whose balustraded parapets are decorated with pedimented tabernacles supporting classical vases and statues, all of which raise these entrance bays to Frontispieces.' (Pevsner, **'Nottinghamshire'**). There are also some elaborate pinnacles or turrets adorning the four towers. An interesting feature are the many circular niches, filled with busts of philosophers and ancient deities, Virgil, Plato, Aristotle and Diana, which decorate the facades of the building.

However, the classicism of Wollaton has been blended with French and Flemish architecture presenting a building amassed with ornamental decoration. As indicated by Summerson, the greatest inspiration behind the Wollaton ornamentation are the Flemish styles represented in **'Variae Architecturae Formae'** by Vredeman de Vries and reflected in the flamboyant strapwork cartouches, particularly of the Dutch gables and the aprons below the windows. Thus Wollaton Hall is composed of a variation of architectural styles. Classical niches and the gondola rings on the dies of the ground floor pilasters are mixed with Venetian styles, such as those seen decorating the tops of the tower windows. The influence of French architecture can be seen in the large pepper pot lids or tourelles adorning the corners of the Prospect Room. To complete such detailed carving, Sir Francis employed some of the best stone masons in the

country. These included such men as Christopher Lovell, John Rodes and Thomas Accres who, in their time, worked at such stately homes as Longleat and Hardwick Hall.

A classical niche filled with the bust of Aristotle, decorating the North Facade of the Hall
Photograph: Elizabeth May

Classical pilasters with Doric capitals enclosing the ground floor windows of Wollaton Hall
Photograph: Elizabeth May

Classical vases and statues supported on pedimented tabernacles which decorate the balustraded parapets of the East and West Fronts of the Hall
Photograph: Elizabeth May

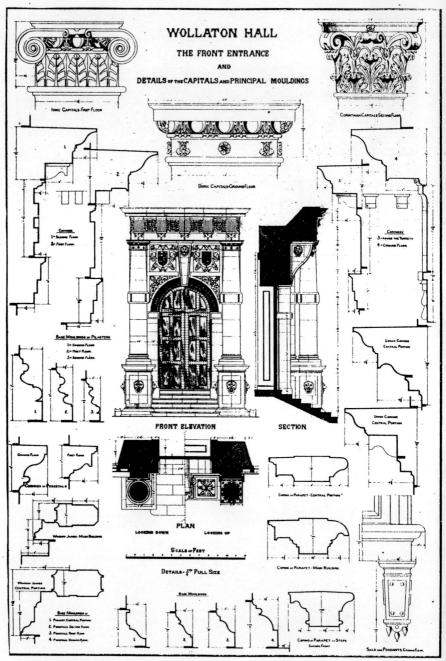

WOLLATON HALL

THE FRONT ENTRANCE

AND

DETAILS of the CAPITALS and PRINCIPAL MOULDINGS

FRONT ELEVATION

SECTION

PLAN

LOOKING DOWN   LOOKING UP

SCALE of FEET

DETAILS · ¼ᵀᴴ FULL SIZE

Measured and Drawn by Mr. Percy K. Allen   Reprinted from *'The Builder'* 1889
Acknowledgement to Nottingham University Library Manuscripts Department

Dutch gables form the top of the corner pavilions which are decorated with strapwork cartouches
Photograph: Elizabeth May

Gondola rings on the bases of the ground floor pilasters
Photograph: Elizabeth May

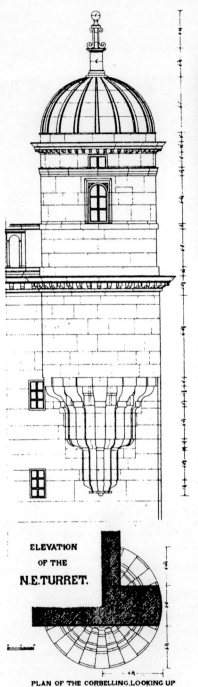

Above: **One of the tourelles or pepper pot lidded turrets adorning the four corners of the Prospect Room, each of which represents a separate little room looking over the surrounding countryside**

Photograph: by permission of the Natural History Museum, Wollaton Hall

Left: **The design of one of the tourelles as drawn by P. K. Allen in the periodical *'The Builder'* in 1889**

Acknowledgement to Nottingham University Library Manuscripts Department

ELEVATION
OF THE
N.E.TURRET.

PLAN OF THE CORBELLING.LOOKING UP

One of the most interesting features of Wollaton is that despite being composed of the latest Flemish and Italian architecture it is also influenced by past medieval styles. Wollaton's design can be associated more with the medieval towered Mount Edgcumbe in Cornwall than with the classicism of Longleat. Indeed its rectangular shape, sturdy corner towers or pavilions and the clerestory lit Central Hall bear a marked resemblence to the former. The influence of Gothic architecture on Wollaton can be seen in the strong perpendicular lines created by the pilasters and mullions which present a contrast to the horizontal emphasis of the parapet and entablature. These stone mullions and transoms in the windows, the tracery on those of the Prospect Room together with the curved decorative grouped chimneys on the tops of the towers, all serve to give Wollaton a definite medieval flavour.

The interior of Wollaton Hall, which now houses the county's Natural History Museum, has undergone considerable alterations since Elizabethan times. Extensive refurbishment took place in the late 17th century after a fire in

Stone mullions and transoms in the windows of the Hall   Photograph: Elizabeth May

An aerial view of one of the
corner pavilions showing
the grouped chimneys and
curved Dutch gables

The clerestory windows of
the Prospect Room which
with their tracery remind
one of Medieval Gothic
architecture

Photographs: by permission of
the Natural History Museum,
Wollaton Hall

1642 and there were also some alterations made by the architect Jeffrey Wyatville in the early 19th century. His plans involved the construction of additional underground servants' quarters on the western side of the building and also the re-designing of the main Entrance Hall.

Originally an L-shaped passage led via stairs from the porch to the Central Hall's Screens Passage. However, Wyatville altered this arrangement and a vestibule now leads one straight from the porch to an entrance in the Central Hall. This raised Central Hall is the main feature of the interior. It is over 50 feet high, is lit by clerestory windows and engulfs the central section of the house. Smythson built the hall above ground level in order to hide the kitchens and servants' quarters underground, so as not to disturb the symmetry of the house. Above its Hammerbeam Timber Roof is a large Prospect Room which provides the third storey of the mansion, and is reached by a little newel staircase situated in two of the corner towers. It is considered that this was used as a Ballroom and it provides some spectacular views of the surrounding countryside in all directions. Another unusual feature in the interior design was the arrangement of the first floor in the form of two matching North and South Great Chambers on either side of the Central Hall. These symmetrical apartments reflect the division between the King's and Queen's apartments seen in Royal Houses in later years. The design suggests that Willoughby hoped that the Queen would honour him with a visit to his splendid new home. Alas, she never came.

Very litttle of the original splendour which once decked the interior of the mansion now remains and its rooms, which once served some of the wealthiest people in England, are now devoted solely to housing the Museum's rich display of Natural History specimens. The arrangement of the ground floor has been little changed to accommodate the Museum, and the exhibits fit comfortably into the various rooms. The large Bone Room now occupies what was once the Reception Lounge or Saloon on the South front.

The Central Hall, its Screens Passage and the Family Dining Room on the west side, are all used for the exhibition of the

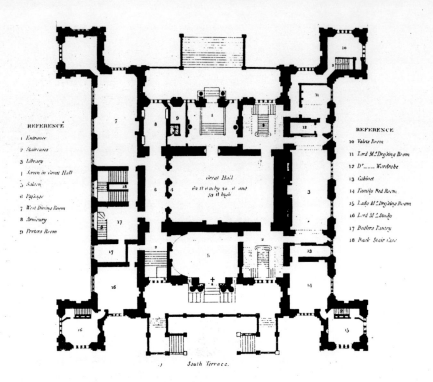

Great Hall

South Terrace.

Acknowledgement to Nottinghamshire County Library Service

Above is a plan by Wyatville showing the interior design of Wollaton Hall in the early 19th century revealing the new vestibule leading from the main North entrance which replaced the L-shaped passage seen in the original Smythson plan right

Acknowledgement to Mark Girouard's book *'Robert Smythson and the Elizabethan Country House'* (1983)

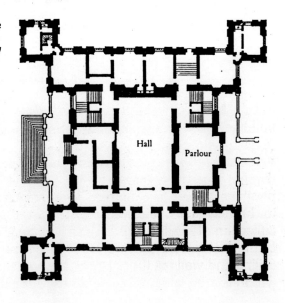

Hall

Parlour

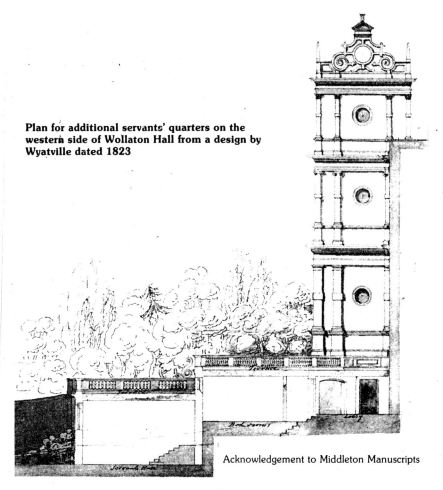

Plan for additional servants' quarters on the western side of Wollaton Hall from a design by Wyatville dated 1823

Acknowledgement to Middleton Manuscripts

Museum's large mammal collection. Much of the original Elizabethan architecture still surviving in the interior of the building can be found in this Great Central Hall, and consists of a large stone Screen situated on the western side of the hall, a Doric Fireplace and the Hammerbeam Roof overlooking the whole. The library on the eastern side of the building previously used to house collections of specimens belonging to Francis the Naturalist is now used to display a large collection of birdlife, which seems wholly appropriate in view of the Naturalist's pioneering work in this subject. While the ceiling and walls of the main north staircase are still beautifully decorated with Baroque paintings, the North and South Great

A section of the Open Hammerbeam Roof, which is painted and carved to look like stone and decorated with shields and corbels. It is not a true Hammerbeam, but is merely for decorative purposes Photograph: Elizabeth May

The Screen at Wollaton above which is a Minstrels Gallery complete with organ
Photograph: Elizabeth May

24

WOLLATON HALL

THE ROOF AND SCREEN OF THE LARGE HALL

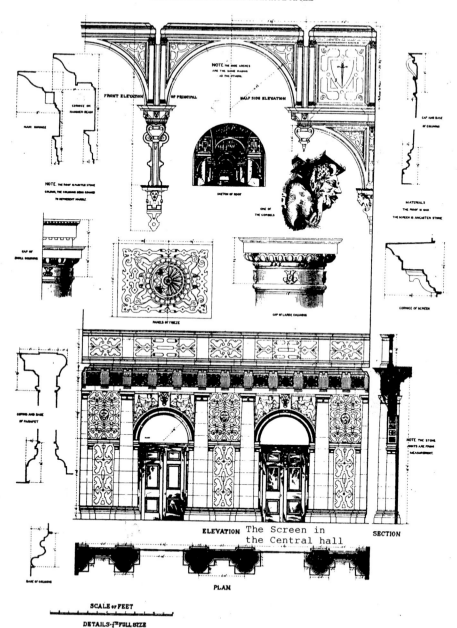

ELEVATION The Screen in the Central hall   SECTION

Measured and Drawn by Mr. Percy K. Allen   Reprinted from *'The Builder'* 1889

Acknowledgement to the Nottingham University Library Manuscripts Department

Photograph: Elizabeth May

On the left is a design for a fireplace in Serlio's *'Architecture'* which has been reproduced in the Central Hall at Wollaton as revealed by the photograph

Acknowledgement to Mark Girouard's book *'Robert Smythson and the Elizabethan Country House'* (1983) and R.I.B.A London

The coat of arms which once adorned the Willoughby family's flag standard with its symbol, the owl, which is appropriate in view of the important contribution the family has made to Natural History

Photograph by permission of the Natural History Museum, Wollaton Hall

Gallery

North Great Chamber

South Great Chamber

A design of the original First Floor Plan showing the two symmetrical North and South Great Chambers and a long Gallery running along the eastern side of this storey

Acknowledgement to Mark Girouard's book 'Robert Smythson and the Elizabethan Country House' (1983)

Chambers and Gallery on the first floor, have for the most part been stripped of their original furnishings and splendour, and now serve to accommodate some large mineral and fossil collections, together with various sea specimens, the Insect Gallery, and the Nottinghamshire Room devoted to local conservation.

The perfect symmetrical design of Wollaton Hall continues into its formal gardens with the Hall occupying a central position overlooking the surrounding parkland in various directions. As can be seen from the Smythson plan, the house, gardens, courtyards and outbuildings all formed a large square. The house was designed to be the central

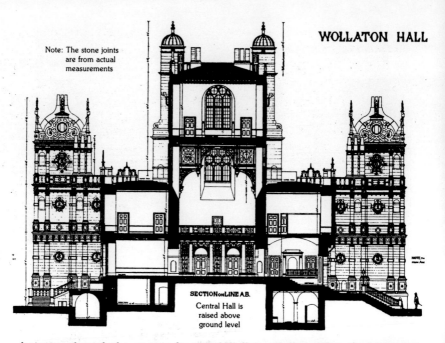

Note: The stone joints
are from actual
measurements

SECTION on LINE A.B.
Central Hall is
raised above
ground level

A section through the western facade of Wollaton Hall revealing the interior of the Central Hall with its Screen and Hammerbeam Timber Roof, above which is the Prospect Room. The kitchens and servants' quarters are clearly visible underground Acknowledgement to Middleton Manuscripts

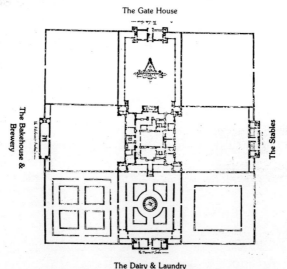

The Gate House

The Bakehouse & Brewery

The Stables

The Dairy & Laundry

Plan of Wollaton Hall, its grounds and outbuildings which formed a large square
Acknowledgement to R.I.B.A. London

building with the gatehouse, stables and various outbuildings all facing it from different directions. Evidence suggests much of this arrangement was carried out, and the remains are clearly visible from a plan dated 1690 found among the Willoughby family documents.

The parkland surrounding Wollaton Hall, which for many centuries was devoted to hunting purposes, today functions as a sanctuary for local wildlife. These lands once extended over an area of 784 acres, which was enclosed by a wall during the late 17th century, although today this has been considerably reduced to c. 400 acres as a result of land development. Among the magnificent trees which are interspersed throughout this undulating landscape, are two avenues of majestic oaks seen from the north facade of the house, which are said to have been sown by the great naturalist Francis Willoughby. There is also an ancient avenue of limes leading

The ceiling above the main North Staircase, *'Prometheus stealing the fire from Heaven,'* Photograph: Elizabeth May

29

**The base of a Doric Column as
represented in *'Das Erst Buch'*
(1565) by Vredeman de Vries**

Acknowledgement to R.I.B.A. London

**The panel in the Screen at
Wollaton above reveals the
influence of de Vries**

**Panel in the Frieze above the
Screen by Smythson**

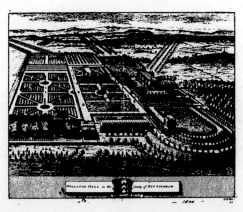

**Plan dated 1690 found among the Willoughby family papers showing Wollaton
Hall and its gardens to the south**   Acknowledgement to Middleton Manuscripts

up towards the Hall from the Lenton Lodge Entrance to the east of the park. Today the extensive lake, woodlands and open pasture areas make Wollaton Park a perfect sanctuary for many varieties of birdlife and a popular grazing ground for herds of Red and Fallow Deer.

The two avenues of oaks sown by Francis Willoughby the Naturalist, leading up to Wollaton Hall's north facade   Photograph: Elizabeth May

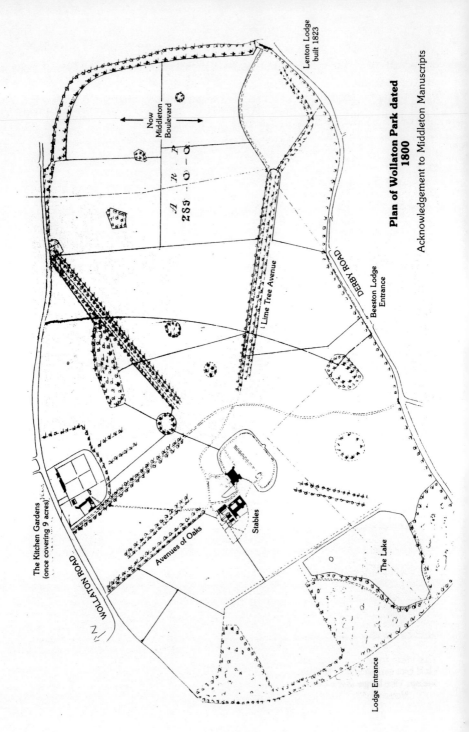

Plan of Wollaton Park dated 1800

Acknowledgement to Middleton Manuscripts

Lenton Lodge built 1823

Now Middleton Boulevard

DERBY ROAD

Beeston Lodge Entrance

Lime Tree Avenue

The Kitchen Gardens (once covering 9 acres)

WOLLATON ROAD

Avenues of Oaks

Stables

The Lake

Lodge Entrance

A. R. O. -O-
289

The view from the west of the Hall overlooking the elegantly landscaped gardens and the lake in the distance
Photograph: Elizabeth May

The view from the south which was originally built as the main entrance to the Hall but which fell into disuse over the years in favour of the North entrance used today. The large lawn contained a line of four life-size statues of Neptune, Mars, Venus with Cupid and Apollo, together with an ornamental fountain

Acknowledgement to D.R.G. J. Arthur Dixon

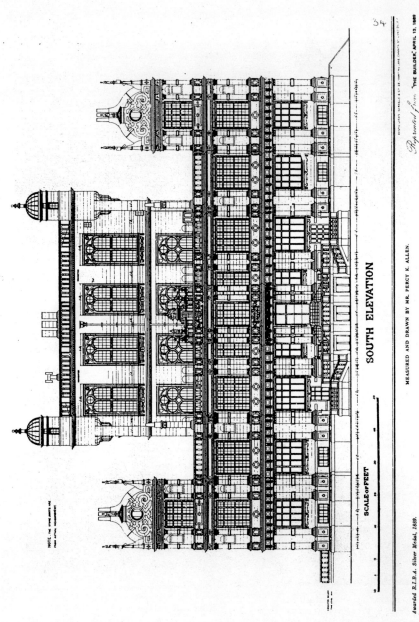

SOUTH ELEVATION

SCALE OF FEET

NOTE. THE STONE JOINTS ARE FROM ACTUAL MEASUREMENT.

MEASURED AND DRAWN BY MR. PERCY K. ALLEN.

Awarded R.I.B.A. Silver Medal, 1889.

Reprinted from "THE BUILDER," APRIL 13, 1889.

Acknowledgement to Nottingham University Library Manuscripts Department

The gardens to the west of the Hall with the magnificent Camellia House constructed in 1823, and which houses some of the finest camellias in the country
Photograph: Elizabeth May

Late seventeenth century Stable Block to the far north-west of the Hall, designed by Francis the Naturalist's elder son, and now houses the Industrial Museum
Photograph: Elizabeth May

FRANCIS WILLOUGHBY THE PIONEER OF NATURAL HISTORY

Through the ages man has shown increasing interest in the world of nature and in the flora and fauna that inhabit his environment. From the time of Moses and through the Medieval Period, much of the work done in this field was either related to ancient myth and legend or was limited to the study of prey for sporting pursuits. The most notable early achievements are attributed to the famous Greek philosopher, Aristotle, who in the 4th century B.C. is credited with being the first to pursue Natural History as a science, and it was to his works which many later Naturalists referred. The great voyages of discovery which took place from the 13th century onwards also served to promote an increasing interest in this field, as man was brought into contact with the natural phenomena of many varied and distant countries.

The first major scientific investigations and discoveries in Natural History occurred on the continent during the 16th century, and the increased interest in the subject was greatly influenced by the Renaissance. C. Raven makes the point that 'the traditional medieval doctrines towards nature and, indeed, life in general, were gradually transcended by more modern attitudes, due to the advent of this new cultural movement.' During the 16th century, the traditional medieval pastimes of hunting and falconry gradually began to decline in popularity, being replaced by new cultural forms of entertainment like the masque, drama and, indeed, horse-racing. Together with these changes came a greater appreciation of the world of nature and a desire for further knowledge of Natural History, which ultimately paved the way for the considerable progress made during the latter part of the 17th century.

Although Britain cannot claim any high place among the early pioneers, great progress was to be made from the mid-17th century with the rise to prominence of such esteemed men as John Ray and Francis Willoughby. Their achievements together with the foundation of the Royal Society in 1662 saw Britain gain a significant reputation in Natural History, and one which was to more than equal that of the rest of Europe for many generations.

Francis Willoughby F.R.S., the eminent Naturalist and Philosopher, was born at Middleton in Warwickshire in 1635, the only son of Sir Francis Willoughby and Cassandra Ridgway, daughter of the Earl of Londonderry. He was descended from two very ancient families of Willoughbys, on his grandfather's side from the Willoughbys of Eresby in Lincolnshire and on his grandmother's from the well known Willoughbys of Wollaton.

After spending his boyhood at Sutton Coldfield school, Francis attended Trinity College, Cambridge in 1653 where he studied a variety of subjects including Architecture, Classical Literature, Mathematics and Botany. He was tutored by James Duport, who had previously taught John Ray the renowned Botanist who, by this date, had become a lecturer himself at the University.

Despite his wealthy background, Willoughby was prepared to work hard for his achievements, so much so that 'his friends were of the opinion that he did much weaken his health by his incessant labours.' However, he was justly rewarded for his efforts, gaining a B.A. in 1655-6 and an M.A. three years later in 1659.

At Cambridge a great friendship began bet-

Francis Willoughby F.R.S. (1635-1672)

38

ween Ray, the talented Botanist and teacher, and his pupil, Willoughby, the learned Zoologist. The two men were to contribute greatly to their respective fields during the 17th century. Though they were from widely different backgrounds, Willoughby being the son of a gentleman and Ray a blacksmith's son, they shared the same ambitions and love of the natural world. Ray undoubtedly encouraged Willoughby's interest in Natural History during his years at Cambridge and during the late 1650s, evidence reveals, that Willoughby was involved in carrying out chemical experiments for Ray. By 1660 Willoughby, having

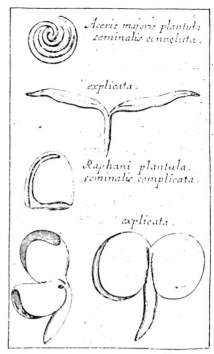

An illustration of a selection of germinating seeds from 'Historia Plantarum'

Acknowledgement to Middleton Manuscripts

decided that his ambitions lay in that direction, was for much of the year involved in research work for Ray, consulting rare books on Natural History at the Bodleian Library in Oxford. His help to Ray, including some early work concerning insects, is acknowledged by Ray in his 1660 'Catalogus Plantarum circa Cantbrigiam.' In February of that year, Ray wrote to Willoughby requesting the latter's help in compiling a more detailed account of rare British plants, saying 'for the counties of Warwickshire and Nottinghamshire, I must beg your assistance,' which is an indication that Willoughby was knowledgeable and had a considerable interest in the Natural History of this county. This letter saw the beginning of a partnership between the two which proved of considerable importance to the development of Natural History on a worldwide scale over the following decade.

Alka Hoieri.
The Razor-bill or Auk.

An illustration of a Razor-bill or Auk from Willoughby's *'Ornithologia'*
Acknowledgement to Middleton Manuscripts

Willoughby was subsequently to accompany Ray on a series of travels which began as a search for botanical specimens, both in Britain and on the continent, and as a result of which the two were able to compile the famous *'Historia Plantarum,'* and also to make some major progress in Zoology. On August 1st 1660, they commenced their first extensive tour through the North of England and the Isle of Man, during which they collected a variety of interesting plants, all of which were eventually included in the first systematic classification of plants, published by Ray in three volumes from 1686 to 1704.

Their early discoveries included such plants as the large Field Garlic *(Allium Oleraceum Var Complanatum),* found in the mountains above Settle in Yorkshire, together with a range of grasses and ferns, including a variety of fern called the Filix Florida, all of which were located on the Isle of Man. On an extensive tour of Wales in 1662, the intrepid Naturalists discovered more valuable botanical specimens. The Columbine *(Aquilegia Vulgaris),* was located by Willoughby 'neere ye wel at Kilkin in Flintshire and about Denbigh,' together with many specimens of rushes found near Harlech.

Even after Willoughby concentrated his interests on Zoology, he still continued to provide Ray with valuable plant specimens which enabled him to complete the *'Historia Plantarum.'* These included a volume of specimens of dried plants obtained from the Botanical Gardens at Padua in Italy,

A Botanical specimen from the Columbine *(Aquilegia Vulgaris)* collected by Willoughby in Wales in 1662

A variety of Meadow Orchid *(Orchis Palmatra Odorata)*, labelled by Ray in *'Historia Plantarum'* as having been found in Wales 'on ye back of Snowdon not farre from Llanberis in ye way from Canarvon'

Amarantus Spicatus Luteus, thought to be a variety of Amaranth collected by Willoughby from the Botanical Gardens at Padua in Italy

Peucedanum Minus located by Philip Skippon on the Calabrian coast of Italy

Acknowledgement to Middleton Manuscripts

together with others collected during the continental tour.

The travels undertaken in 1662 through Wales and the North Midland Counties were very important as they inspired Willoughby and Ray to embark on a comprehensive study of Natural History, and thus to lay the foundations for future research. During their travels through Wales, they came into contact with many different aspects of nature and realised together that there was a definite lack of documentation on the subject. To combat this, the two men, before their travels on the continent, decided in the words of Ray, 'to reduce the several tribes of things to a method, and to give accurate descriptions of the several species from a strict view of them .' Thus, as Willoughby's interest was inclined towards Zoology, he undertook a study of the animals, fish and insects inhabiting the earth, while Ray in Botany.

The rich variety of birdlife and fish found on the tour of Wales enabled Willoughby to increase his knowledge of Zoology and many of the species located were ultimately described in his major works 'Ornithologia' and 'Historia Piscium.' It was at Prestholm, which is now named Puffin Island, where the birdlife particularly interested Willoughby, and he was able to observe two different varieties of Gulls, together with Cormorants, Puffins, Quillems and Scrays. He also observed some Razor-bills which he had previously studied on the Isle of Man.

The small islands around the Welsh coast were rich in birdlife and on the Isle of Bardsey, Willoughby was able to discover the Prestholm Puffin's nesting place and also to study some Oystercatchers. 'Historia Piscium,' published in 1686 included a great many varieties of fish, some of which were first observed by Willoughby in the Welsh town of Tenby, where besides the common species of Cod, Mackerel and Hake, he also saw Shark, together with many Shellfish.

Willoughby's new scientific purpose was to be fulfilled in the continental travels that he made with Ray between 1663 and 1664, when they discovered more information in their respective fields than any previous known scientists, and which were to enable them to produce the world's first complete systematic classifications of both plants and animals.

In the spring of 1663, Ray and Willoughby undertook a tour of the continent accompanied by Philip Skippon and Nathaniel Bacon, two former pupils of Ray's at Cambridge. Their journey took them through part of the Low Countries, Germany, Switzerland, Italy and France, with further exploration by Francis Willoughby in Spain.

It was during their travels through Germany and especially along the Danube and the Rhine that Willoughby acquired much valuable information concerning Zoology, together with some beautiful hand-engraved illustrations, some of which graced the pages of **'Ornithologia'** and **'Historia Piscium.'**

At Strasbourg, Willoughby bought from a fisherman, Leonard Baltner, a collection of pictures of the different waterfowl, fish and water insects found along the Rhine. A few months later at Nuremberg, he purchased a further collection featuring birds drawn in colour. One of the most interesting discoveries made by Willoughby on this tour came in Vienna where, in the market place, he was able to see the large Silurus or Sheat-fish, described by Ray as the 'greatest of all fresh water fish that we have seen.'

It is indeed unfortunate that all the written notes compiled by Ray and Willoughby on the continent were lost on their return to England, an incident which served to render Willoughby's work on fishes much less complete than he would have desired. However, Willoughby gathered a varied collection of stuffed birds, fishes, fossils and seeds on his travels which were kept in Wollaton's Library for many years. The seed collection is now housed at Birdsall in N. Yorkshire, home of the present Lord Middleton.

Some of Willoughby's most important research work was performed at Padua in Italy during the winter of 1663-64 where he became familiar with the technique of dissection and also undertook studies in Comparative Anatomy. Some of the most important research over the last century had been carried out at this famous university, including comparisons between the bone structure of the human body and that of animals and birds. Indeed studies of this nature were still continuing well into the second half of the 17th century. It was to this school that the famous Italian scientist Malpighi

William Morice Knt. One of his ——
Ma.ties most Honorable Privy Councell,
and Principall Secretary of State.

You are vpon sight hereof to suffer the Bearers
Francis Willoughby Esq.re & Nathaniel Bacon Gent.
with two Seruants, their wearing apparill, & other
necessaries, freely to passe beyond the Seas, for their
experience & improuement by Trauill; Prouided ——
they carry no prohibited goods, and do all such things,
and giue all such cautions as by the Lawes & Statutes
of this Realme of England are in that case required
and prouided for: And you are in like manner to
suffer them & either of them to returne againe when
their occasions shall require, without any lett, ——
hindrance or molistacon. Hereof you are not to ——
faile; And for so doing this shall be your Warrant.
Giuen at Whitehall the Tenth day of April, 1663.

To all Captains of his Ma.ties Shipps
at Sea, Gouernors, Comandors, Souldiers,
Maiors, Sheriffs, Justices of the Peace,
Bailiffs, Constables, Customers, ——
Comptrollers, Searchers, or others whom
it may Concerne.

Will Morice

**Passport belonging to Willoughby, Bacon and two servants dated at Whitehall
16th April 1663 two days before they embarked on the continental tour**
Acknowledgement to Middleton Manuscripts

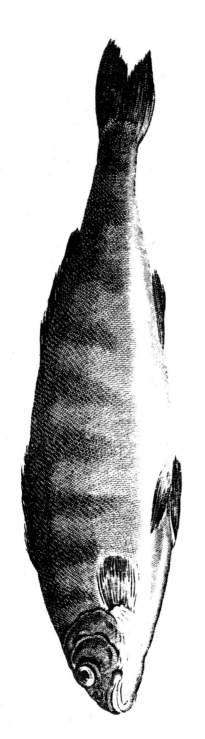

Illustration of Perch from *'Historia Piscium'* which was part of the collection by Leonard Baltner, purchased by Willoughby at Strasbourg

Acknowledgement to Nottinghamshire County Library Service

belonged

At the university, Willoughby and his fellow travellers were able to attend lectures in anatomy given by Pietro Marchetti, and also to witness a human dissection performed on a woman's body at the Marchetti house. It was here that Willoughby learnt the importance of dissection in research of Natural History, which proved very useful in his study of the internal parts of birds.

The major importance of Willoughby's Spanish tour in August 1664 was that it presented an opportunity to increase his knowledge of Whales on which he compiled the first accurate information in his 'Historia Piscium.' Before Willoughby's time, the Whale was viewed as a mythical creature rarely seen by man and about which little information was known. Francis Willoughby was the first Naturalist to provide accurate descriptions, together with some drawings, of the commoner species of Whale, including the Atlantic Right Whale, which is now regarded as a rare species. He had already acquired some knowledge of these mammals before his Spanish tour, much of which can be attributed to the accounts brought back by early explorers, together with information he obtained from whales occasionally washed up on British shores.

In Spain, he was able to gather information concerning certain whales, including a species known as the Sperma Ceti. which became stranded in the shallow waters off the coast of Bayonne and St. Sebastian. In his account of the Spanish tour, Willoughby expresses his knowledge relating to the habits of these mammals, stating that 'Every winter, there are several whales caught upon this coast, they coming hither in winter and frequenting heer, as they do upon the coast of Greenland in summer.'

Willoughby's great contribution to Natural History was in the formation of a system of classification. This system is demonstrated in his first major work 'Ornithologia,' which John Ray was to complete after Willoughby's death in 1672. The importance of this to future Naturalists is indicated by the fact that Linnaeus himself, who did so much for the advancement of this science during the 18th century, based

**Illustration of a Fish related to the
Sharks and Rays from *'Historia
Piscium'* for which Samuel Pepys
provided 60 engravings of fishes**
Acknowledgement to Nottinghamshire
County Library Service

47

CO. PAVLVS BE BENNASSVTVS VICENTINVS

IN ALMA VNIVERSITATE DD. IVRISTARVM VRISTARVM PATAVINI ARCHIGYMNASII PRORECTOR, AOR. AC SYNDICVS

CVM SINGVLARVM NATIONVM NATIONVM CONSILIARIIS

VNIVERSIS, ET SINGVLIS fidem facimus, & attestamur, quod infrascriptus est noster Scolasticus, scriptus in Matricula, & ob id gaudet omnibus, & quibuscunque Priuileg. quibuscunque Priuilegijs, immunitatibus scolasticis, & exemptionibus Dationum Almæ nostræ Vniuersitati concessis, â Sereniss. Dominio Venetiarum, Dominio Venetoatque in nostro libro Scarttorij insertis. Ipsum propterea immunem, ac exemptum pariter, & omnia bona, famulos, nuncinia bona, famulos,nunciosque suos esse volumus, ab omni Datij, Gabellæ, Regalium, & quarumcunque Repræsaliarum solutione. Horramur itaque, & præsentium tenore iubemus, omnes & singulos Datij Præsidentes, Datiarios, eorumque Ministros, Officiales, præterfritros, præsertim Ciuitatis, Venetiarum, Fluminum Palacerios, Portiones quarumlibet Ciuitatum, Portarum Custodes Sereniss. Duc. Dominij Ventorum, vt infrâ scriptum, famulos, & nuncios suos cum bonis, & rebus, tam mobilibus, quàm e mouentibus cuiuscunque generis, & conditionis pro se, & familiæ suæ vsu necessarijs, & honorificis, ad Ciuitatem hanc venire, transire, redire, emere, conducere, vendere, absq; alicuius Datij, Gabellæ, Regalium, Portiorij, transitus Pontium, Repræsaliaruontium, Repræsalaruonium, & introitus solutione, permittant ; Etiamsi vina tranlucherentur huc, aut emerentur alienæ vinæ, vel Territorij, quam Patauini. Quæ omnia de iure, & ex nostrorum Statuorum forma facere tenentur, obligatiq; sunt sub pœna librarum centum pœna librarum centum, &c. Pro præmissorum autem execution iuxta eadem Statura requirimus omnes, & singulos Illustriss. DD. Rectores Vrbium, ac locorum omnium Sereniss. orum omnium Sereniss. Dominij, vt prædicta priuilegia, & hæc præcepta nostra prout iacent obseruent, & inuiolabiliter obseruari præcipiant. In quorum fidem has nostras per infrâ scriptum Cancellarium postreum fieri, cellarium postreum fieri, & nostrę Vniuersitatis solito sigillo communiri iussimus.

Dat. Patauij in Offic. Vniuersitatis Iuristarum, Die 17 Mense _____ & Anno 16__ inno 16__

NOI PAOLO BENNASSVTI vel Alma Vniuersità de' Sig. Leggisti nesista de' Sig. Leggisti nel celebre Studio di Padua PRORETTORE, e SINDICO, con i Consiglieri di ciascuna Nazione, facciamo à tutti, & ciascuno, che vedreano la presani indubitata fede, & attestiamo ...

R. 3. coll. Libri —

N.403

his Ornithological Classification on Willoughby's system.

Willoughby's *'Ornithologia'* is divided into three books or sections, the first being a study of birds in general, with details of both their internal and external structure and appearance, together with their age, size, colour and the various hatching out processes of their young. The second book deals with birds living on land and the third with water fowl, distinguishing between the waders and the birds which actually swim. Naturally, Willoughby on his travels was unable to observe every bird mentioned and in order to complete the work, Ray gathered information from the books of other Naturalists around the world. The various species of bird are accurately distinguished in great detail and the whole forms the most complete and accurate classification of birds written by any scientist at the time. The book was published first in Latin in 1675 and then in English three years later. It is to this English edition that Ray added three discourses — comprising of a section on singing birds, on the management and training of hawks for Falconry and also information concerning the art of Fowling. Pressure from the demands of the time appears to have led to the inclusion of the information on hunting of birds, though to the modern reader, this subject may not appear to be in keeping with the idea of Natural History,

Anser Canadensis
The Canada Goose

The Canada Goose as pictured in *'Ornithologia'*, which is thought of as a relatively modern bird, but which was, in fact first discovered in Willoughby's time
Acknowledgement to Middleton Manuscripts

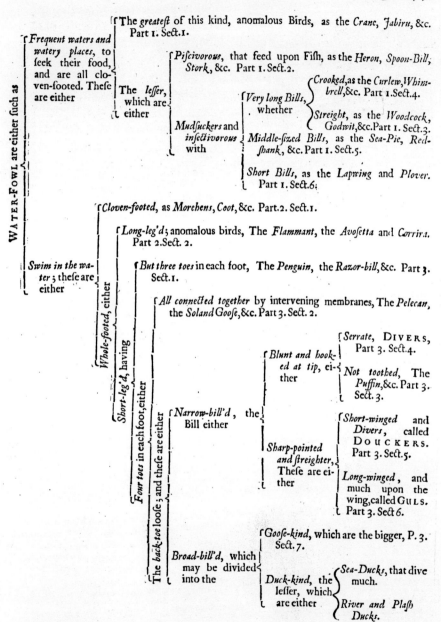

Willoughby's Table of Waterfowl distinguishing between the wading birds and those that swim
Acknowledgement to Middleton Manuscripts

Illustration on the trapping of birds in Willoughby's *'Ornithologia'*
Acknowledgements to Middleton Manuscripts

which has become increasingly involved with conservation, and seeks to preserve existing species of wildlife for future generations to enjoy.

Willoughby, despite concentrating on aspects of Zoology, had maintained an interest in Botany and it was this, together with his research on insects, which filled his attention in the latter years of his life.

On his return from the continent, Willoughby entered upon a course of enquiries into the theory of vegetation in the winter of 1664-65, in an attempt to discover whether a circulatory process similar to that of blood in animals, existed in the constitution of plants.

In the spring of 1669, he expanded these enquiries with the help of his colleague, Ray. Experimenting on a variety of trees, including Birch, Maple and Oak, of different ages and under different climatic conditions, Willoughby reached the conclusion that there was a solidifying of sap similar to the clotting of blood, but no circulatory process as such.

Willoughby's entomological discoveries, like his zoological studies, were foundations for future research. His observations on the insect world date back to his research on caterpillars while at the Bodleian Library in 1660. In the last two years of his life, 1670 and 1671, he undertook research into many different insects including a type of wasp named *Vespae Ichneumones*.

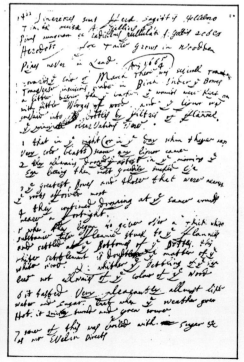

A page from Francis Willoughby's Commonplace Book recording experiments conducted on the rising of sap in Birch trees, dated 1664/65

Acknowledgements to Middleton Manuscripts

Part of his work, published in the *Royal Society's 'Philosophical Transactions,'* described how the maggot of the wasp lives and grows inside caterpillars. Other information worth relating concerned the hatching of a type of 'Bee lodged in old Willows' *(Philosophical Transactions, No. 74)*.

Unfortunately, due to his untimely death at the age of 37, Willoughby was unable to complete his enquiries in this field and his great colleague, John Ray, completed and published all Willoughby's research in three major works, *'Ornithologia,' 'Historia Piscium,'* and *'Historia Insectorum'* at intervals over the following thirty years, thus providing future generations with the first comprehensive classification in Zoology.

THE MODERN FUNCTION OF WOLLATON HALL

Wollaton Hall functions as a Natural History Museum providing information for the general public, and as a centre for the preservation of local wildlife around Nottinghamshire. The Hall, however, was not the original site for the Natural History Museum, which from 1874 was based at the Architectural and Natural Sciences Library on Shakespeare Street in Nottingham's City Centre. It was not until the purchase of Wollaton Hall by Nottingham Corporation in 1925 that the building was converted to its present use which nowadays, in cooperation with organisations such as the Nottinghamshire Wildlife Trust, works to safeguard wildlife and its natural habitats. One cannot help but feel that it is indeed a fitting tribute to the achievements of the eminent Naturalist, Francis Willoughby, that this stately home should finally become the centre for the area's Natural History Museum.

In Willoughby's lifetime Natural History was a new area of discovery not associated with conservation. Very little accurate documentary evidence had been recorded on the subject before the middle of the 17th century, and much is owed to Willoughby and his colleague Ray, for the formulation of a complete system of classification for both Zoology and Botany. Indeed it was this achievement which paved the way for the in-depth research carried out by later generations.

Today the work done in the Biological Records Section at the Hall, where all local information on Natural History is stored and analysed, can be paralleled with Willoughby's search for knowledge. It consists of two major collections both for the information of the general public, to stimulate the protection of wildlife, and to encourage safeguarding rare species. One collection is comprised purely of botanical and zoological specimens while the second is an archive of information on the many aspects of nature in the Nottingham area and, worldwide.

Much local information is provided by volunteer groups undertaking field surveys for the Nottinghamshire Trust, the results of which are analysed and stored for future reference. Technological developments have led to the introduction of a computerised system of classification, which is a considerable advancement on that of Willoughby and Ray. The recent

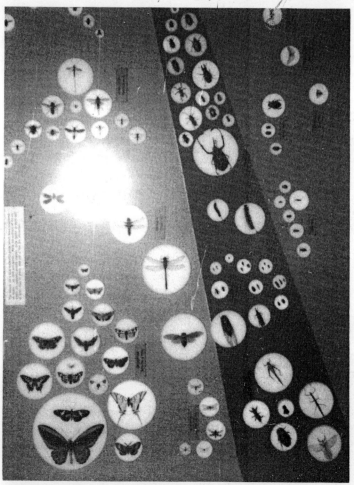

A selection of Beetles and winged insects on display in the Museum's Insect Gallery   Photograph: Elizabeth May

computerisation of information on all known British plants, as well as a great many foreign varieties, is proving a great asset allowing speedy and easy access to information.

The Museum has an extensive collection of zoological specimens, some of which are extremely rare, with a selection of these being on permanent exhibition for the general public. The latter provide a good general knowledge of the various forms of life inhabiting the earth. However, the bulk of the Museum's extensive collection is kept in storage in various parts of the building. The number of vertebrates alone in the collection is estimated at 20,000, consisting of a range of mammals, birds, fish, amphibians and reptiles, together with 40,000 birds' eggs. There is also an extensive insect collection, including specimens of Butterflies and Moths, Snails and an impressive Beetle collection, ranging from the smallest British specimens to the large continental varieties. A selection of such specimens are on permanent exhibition in the Museum's Insect Gallery, where there is an observation Bee-Hive and Ant Colony.

Many of the Hall's specimens are extremely old, having been acquired by the first curator of the original Museum, Professor Carr, between 1890 and 1910. Others were donated to or purchased by the Museum in later years. Many of the rarities among the collection are not part of the Hall's permanent exhibition and include a collection of birds belonging to the local Naturalist, Mansfield Parkyn, collected on his travels to Abyssinia and dating back to 1850. Among them is the first Shoebill ever to be brought into this country in 1802. There are also 14 cases of birds which formed part of the Duke of Portland's collection dated 1850-1860, which contain such rarities as the Alpine Swift, the Bee-Eater and the Peregrine Falcon.

The Museum's permanent exhibition of birdlife, is compiled very much along the lines of Willoughby's early studies and ranges from the common local varieties to the brilliantly coloured tropical species. It includes information on garden birds, sea birds, those inhabiting inland waters and birds of prey, together with species rare to Nottinghamshire such as the Osprey and the Bittern. The Museum distinguishes, as

Willoughby did, between those native to this country and foreign visitors, describes their behaviour patterns, feeding habits, beak differentiations and the way that they are used The exhibits usually include both male and female species of birds with eggs displayed in a diorama of their natural habitat.

It is interesting to note that the Cormorant and the Puffin are given special prominence, for both birds were avidly described by Willoughby in his *'Ornithologia,'* completed after his travels to Puffin Island and the Isle of Man.

Despite its vast collection, the Museum is constantly seeking to further its knowledge, especially concerning the more obscure aspects of nature. The Biological Records Section is currently concerned with Entomology which intrigued Francis the Naturalist in his day, and some of which still remains a mystery to modern man. More information is especially needed on the smaller orders of insects, groups like the Collembloa, which includes the varieties of minute insects, such as Spring Tails, whose natural habitat is found beneath rocks.

Wollaton Hall is also the home of one of the country's leading Taxidermist services which cooperates with the Biological Records Section. By dissection a Taxidermist is able to determine a specimen's age, sex and cause of death. He examines the stomach contents. Any parasites carried by the specimen are analysed and the information gathered is added to records maintained at the Museum.

Don Sharpe, the Museum's Taxidermist, has an outstanding reputation and students come from as far away as Malaysia and Burma specifically to learn his craft. The Taxidermist works in preserving both the Museum's existing collection for posterity, and also in providing additional specimens of wildlife from the local environment. Taxidermists today deal only with natural or road deaths, unlike their predecessors in the late 1800s who recognised the value of a rare bird by shooting it and giving it pride of place in a landowner's mansion.

The specimens are treated either of two ways — mounted for exhibition or used to make a Study Skin, in order to observe such aspects, as pelt colouration in bats.

The Museum's permanent exhibition offers a variety of information at both a local and worldwide level. The exhibition ranges from a large selection of mammals, to a variety of more obscure marine flora and fauna. It even covers aspects of Geology, and has impressive mineral and fossil collections. Thus it can be appreciated that it is designed to appeal to a wide range of interests.

The ground floor exhibits range from a variety of fish and British birds to the more exotic kinds of wildlife from Australia, America and Africa, the most impressive of which is a large Giraffe which stands in the centre of the Great Hall.

Wollaton Hall is one of the few museums in the country with a section devoted entirely to British mammals. A specific 'Wollaton' interest is stimulated by a photographic exhibition

The parrot is representative of a Full Mount complete with glass eyes for exhibition purposes. The bat is a Study Skin filled with cotton wool with a skull labelled for scientific purposes   Photograph: Elizabeth May

Pike displayed in a diorama as part of the Museum's fish collection. The specimens consist of plaster cast moulds on top of which the fishes skin is placed. It is interesting to compare these fish with the Pike illustrated in Willoughby's *'Historia Piscium'*, on the following page   Photograph: Elizabeth May

From left to right, a Spoonbill, a Curlew and an Avocet, together with a description of their various types of beak. Part of the Museum's bird collection
Photograph: Elizabeth May

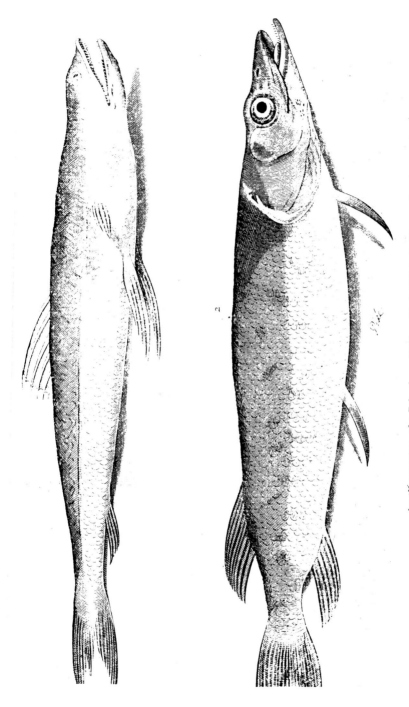

An illustration of a Pike from Willoughby's *'Historia Piscium'*
Acknowledgement to Nottinghamshire County Library Service

tracing the life cycle through the seasons of the park's Red and Fallow Deer, some of which are believed to be descendants of the ancient herd belonging to Sir Francis Willoughby, the builder. Specific local information is also provided here for prospective anglers and birdwatchers, advising on the best coarse and game fishing in the district, and the varieties of birds inhabiting Wollaton Park Lake.

One is reminded of the early anatomical discoveries made at the University of Padua during the 17th century on studying the exhibition of Comparative Anatomy in the Museum's Bone Room. Here the bone structure and layout of a human is set

The Museum's largest exhibit, a Giraffe standing in the Great Central Hall
Photograph: Elizabeth May

against those of apes, birds, rodents and reptiles. One cannot help but feel that the dissection of a pigeon preserved in this section would have appealed greatly to Francis Willoughby.

The Museum plays an important additional role in conservation as a source of information to several organisations including the Nottinghamshire Trust and the Nature Conservancy Council, both of which carry responsibility for the environment.

The Trust is a voluntary body established in 1963. Its 1989 membership stands at 2,500 and the Trust manages 50 Nature Reserves around the county including, Treswell Wood in East Retford and Martin's Pond in Wollaton. Information about the reserves and their specific scientific relevance is stored in the Museum's data bank.

Information is also distributed to the County District Planning Authority, the Severn Trent Water Authority and to landowners. They are advised on the various protected sites and of ways to safeguard them by curtailing industrial development in the areas.

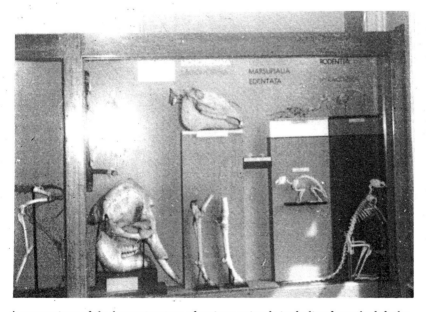

A comparison of the bone structure of various animals including from the left the skull of an Elephant, a Horse together with two of its legs, a Rabbit and a Bennett's Wallaby to the far right   Photograph: Elizabeth May

The museum staff also perform an important public function by assisting with the identification of rare botanical and animal species. Any special information is sent to the Nature Conservancy Council for inclusion in their records of unusual discoveries around Nottinghamshire.

Educational groups are organised to promote an interest in Natural History and there are displays to alert the public to the ever increasing problems of industrial pollution and so forth.

Regular lectures are held for the benefit of the general public which sometimes advise of the relevance of the work of Ray and Willoughby.

The Taxidermy service provides an invaluable aid to the visually handicapped by making available exhibits which visitors may handle — an experience they would otherwise have to forego.

An Ostrich and its young displayed in the Museum's Bone Room, together with a dissection of a Pigeon preserved in the specimen jars   Photograph: Elizabeth May

Other displays are concerned with Nottingham's changing environment and the county's development from the Ice Age to the present century and assess the effect that man has had on the region by coalmining and afforestation projects.

In other parts of the Museum there is information about various endangered species around the world including pythons, crocodiles and elephants. There are also warnings to the public about the illegal importation of skins or tusks of such animals. A considerable number of contraband skins arrive for identification every day, from airports around the country.

There is also information relating to whales of the world which makes it interesting to note that the Atlantic Right Whale first described by Willoughby in his 'Historia Piscium,' is now regarded as an extremely rare species.

In the lifetime of Francis Willoughby, man posed a relatively limited threat to the environment in which he lived. The universe and a great number of living things were still to be discovered, studied and marvelled at. Unfortunately the growth of industrial civilization has often served to isolate man from natural things, and unwittingly destroy them.

However, the achievements of the Willoughby family, Francis the builder and Francis the Naturalist are still with us The former bequeathed his monument to the wealth and grandeur of the past, an achievement acknowledged in the 1988 400th anniversary celebrations of the building of Wollaton Hall. The magnificent building also serves as a constant reminder of the work of Francis the Naturalist, who is still regarded by many as the pioneer of Natural History.

During 1989 changes were made in the arrangement of the Museum, including the introduction of a Period Room in place of the Bone Room, and a room in honour of Francis the Naturalist in recognition of his work.

BIBLIOGRAPHY

Manuscript Source	Title	Location	Ref.
University of Nottingham (Arts Library)	Middleton Manuscripts 5 letters of recommendation written by Merchants in favour of Francis Willoughby for his journey into Spain and dated 1663-1664	Local Studies Dept.	mi/149a/ 2,1-5
University of Nottingham (Arts Library)	Ray, J. 'Observations Topographical Moral and Physiological made in a Journey through Part of the Low Countries etc.' dated in the mid-17th century	Local Studies	mi/LP/33
,, ,,	Ray, J. 'Historia Plantarum' 3 volumes 1686-1704	Local Studies	mi/LM/ 17-24
University of Nottingham (Arts Library)	Willoughby, F. 'Commonplace Note Book' 1658-65	Local Studies	mi/L-M/15
,, ,,	Letter concerning Willoughby's achievements written by Oxford University during 1700s	Local Studies	mi/L-M/15
University of Nottingham (Science Library)	Dr. Derhams 'Life of Ray' dated 1718	Rare Books	QH31.R2
,, ,,	Willoughby, F. 'The Ornithology of Francis Willoughby' (English Edition) dated 1678	Rare Books (oversize)	QL673
Central Library Nottingham (Arts Dept.)	Willoughby, F. 'Historia Piscium' 1686	Rare Books XL85	592.D2

PRINTED SOURCES

du Cerceau J. A.	'Premier Livre'		1559
The Royal Society	'Philosophical Transactions'	No. 74 1671	
The Royal Society	'Philosophical Transactions'	No. 70 1671	
The Royal Society	'Philosophical Transactions'	No. 76 1671	

NEWSPAPERS

Cooke C. H.	Article called 'Willoughby and Wolley Notts Associations of Famous Naturalists'		1945
Granby J.	Article concerning the Willoughbys called 'Local Notes and Queries'		1952

CONTEMPORARY WORKS

Evelyn J.	'Evelyn Sylva'		1664
Historical Manuscripts Commission, Middleton Manuscripts			1702

LATER WORKS

Allen P. K.	'The Builder' (Periodical)	London	1889
Bailey P.	'Annals of Nottinghamshire'	Vol. 3	1928
Dictionary of National Biography Vol. XXI		London	
Fyfe W. W.	'Rambles Round Nottingham'	London	1856
Girouard M.	'Robert Smythson and the Elizabethan Country House'		1983
Jardine W.	'Naturalists Library' Vol. 5	Edinburgh	1843
Lankester E.	'Memorials of John Ray'	London	1846
Miall L. C.	'The Early Naturalists Their Lives and Works'	London	1912
Pevsner N.	'Nottinghamshire'		1951
Raven C. E.	'John Ray Naturalist His Life and Works'	Camb. Uni. Press	1950
Raven C. E.	'English Naturalists from Neckham to Ray'	Camb. Uni. Press	1947
Ray Society	'Correspondence of John Ray'	London	1848
Rossell P.	'The Building of Wollaton Hall'		1957
Smith R. S.	'The Willoughbys of Wollaton 1500-1643'		1964
Society of Architectural Historians	'Architectural History' Vol. 5 (Collection of Drawings by Smythson from the Gotch Catalogue)	London	1962
Strauss S. M.	'A Short History of Wollaton and Wollaton Hall'	Notts. C. C.	1978
Summerson J.	'The Elizabethan Architects' (Article from the 'Book of Architecture' by John Thorpe in Sir John Soane's Museum)	Walpole Society	1978
Holland-Walker J.	'Transactions of the Thoroton Society' Vol 47	Nottingham	1943
Welch M. A.	'Journal for the Society for the Bibliography of Natural History' Vol 6		1972
Welch M. A.	'Transactions of the Thoroton Society' Vol. 81		1977
Wood A. C.	'The Continuation of the History of the Willoughby Family by Cassandra Duchess of Chandos'		1958

ACKNOWLEDGEMENTS

Thanks are extended to the following, for their helpful information which proved useful in compiling this publication. The History Department of the Derbyshire College of Higher Education, the Curator and Staff at Wollaton Hall Museum, the present Lord Middleton, the University of Nottingham Library Manuscripts Department, Nottinghamshire Wildlife Trust and Nottinghamshire County Library Service.

The Nottinghamshire Heritage Series -

BELL TALES by Stan Smith
SOME NOTTINGHAMSHIRE PUB STORIES by Stan Smith
RHYME AND REASON - some Nottinghamshire Folk Tales by Stan Smith

FOR CONSPICUOUS GALLANTRY - Local V.C. Holders - by N. McCrery

HISTORY OF SUTTON IN ASHFIELD - facsimile of 1907 edition

LORD BYRON" Mad, bad and dangerous to know."- by E. Eisenberg

NOTTINGHAMSHIRE STREET TO STREET GUIDE .

THE OLD NORTH ROAD by Joan Board
A TO Z OF PILGRIM COUNTRY by Joan Board

WOLLATON HALL by Elizabeth May
Wollaton as a family home and Natural History Museum

COUNTRY POETRY by Leslie Williamson

NOTTINGHAM IN VERSE - "The Soul of the City" by Alsion Davies

MARY & WILLIAM - a north Midland couple by Joy Dunicliff

BASFORD - Village to Suburb by A.S.Bowley
RAILWAYS REMEMBERED - Basford & Bulwell - 1848 - 1967 by Ashley R. Durose.

LOOKING UP AT NOTTINGHAM - 9 historical city walks by Terence White

For a free catalog of titles
- more than 300 - please write to -

Walk & Write Ltd.,
Unit 1, Molyneux Business Park,
Whitworth Road, Darley Dale,
Matlock, Derbyshire. DE4 2HJ